P9-BJR-395

WITHDRAWN

NOTE TO PARENTS

Welcome to Kingfisher Readers! This program is designed to help young readers build skills, confidence, and a love of reading as they explore their favorite topics.

These tips can help you get more from the experience of reading books together. But remember, the most important thing is to make reading fun!

Tips to Warm Up Before Reading

- Ask your child to share what they already know about the topic.
- Preview the pages, pictures, sub-heads, and captions, so your reader will have an idea what is coming.
- Share your questions. What are you both wondering about?

While Reading

- Stop and think at the end of each section. What was that about?
- Let the words make pictures in your minds. Share what you see.
- When you see a new word, talk it over. What does it mean?
- Do you have more questions? Wonder out loud!

After Reading

- Share the parts that were most interesting or surprising.
- Make connections to other books, similar topics, or experiences.
- Discuss what you'd like to know more about. Then find out!

With five distinct levels and a wealth of appealing topics, the Kingfisher Readers series provides children with an exciting way to learn to read about the world around them. Enjoy!

Ellie Costa, M.S. Ed.
Literacy Specialist, Bank Street School for Children, New York

level
5

Explorers

Chris Oxlade

KINGFISHER
NEW YORK

KINGFISHER
LONDON & NEW YORK

Copyright © Kingfisher 2014
Published in the United States by Kingfisher.
175 Fifth Ave., New York, NY 10010
Kingfisher is an imprint of Macmillan Children's Books, London.
All rights reserved.

Series editor: Polly Goodman
Literacy consultant: Ellie Costa, Bank Street College, New York

ISBN: 978-0-7534-7126-5 (HB)
ISBN: 978-0-7534-7127-2 (PB)

Kingfisher books are available for special promotions and
premiums. For details contact: Special Markets Department,
Macmillan, 175 Fifth Ave., New York, NY 10010.

For more information, please visit
www.kingfisherbooks.com

Printed in China
9 8 7 6 5 4 3 2 1
1TR/1013/WKT/UG/105MA

Picture credits
The Publisher would like to thank the following for permission to reproduce their material. Every care has
been taken to trace copyright holders. However, if there have been unintentional omissions or failure to trace
copyright holders, we apologize and will, if informed, endeavor to make corrections in any future edition.
(t = top; b = bottom; c = center; r = right; l = left):
Cover Kingfisher Archive (KF); Apollo Program/NASA; KF; Shutterstock (SS)/ Alex Staroseltsev; 2l Corbis/
Imaginechina; 2cl KF; 2c NASA; 2cr KF; 2r KF; 3l KF; 3cl KF; 3c Alamy/World History Archive; 3cr Corbis/
Tui De Roy; 3r KF; 4 KF; 5r Alamy/Tetra Images; 6l Corbis/Monalyn Gracia; 7 KF; 8t KF; 8b KF; 9 KF;
10 KF; 11t Corbis/Sakamoto Photo Research laboratory; 11b Corbis/Imaginechina; 12 KF; 13cr KF;
13br KF; 14 KF; 15t KF; 15b SS/Yuri Yavnik; 16cl SS/Uryadnikov Sergey; 16–17 KF; 17cr SS/Loule
Schoeman; 18–19 KF; 19 KF; 20 Getty/Universal History Archive; 21cr KF; 21tr KF; 21b SS/Dolnikov
Denys; 22–23 KF; 24 KF; 25t KF; 25bl Alamy/Mary Evans; 25br Alamy/Simon Grosset; 26–27 KF;
27b KF; 28–29 KF; 29t Alamy/Classic Image; 30 KF; 31t Alamy/Mary Evans; 31b Alamy/Lebrecht
Collection; 32 KF; 33t KF; 33b Alamy/World History Archive; 34 KF; 35 KF; 36–37 KF; 36 KF; 37 KF;
38 Corbis/Bettmann; 39t Alamy/RGS; 39b Corbis/Tui De Roy; 40 KF; 41t Corbis/HO/Reuters; 42 Apollo
Program/NASA; 43t Apollo Program/NASA; 43b Apollo Program/NASA; 44 Corbis/Stephen Frink/Science
Faction; 45t KF; Apollo Program/NASA; 46l Corbis/Imaginechina; 46cl KF; 46c NASA; 46cr KF; 46r KF;
47l KF; 47cl KF; 47c Alamy/World History Archive; 47cr Corbis/Tui De Roy; 47r KF.

Contents

Life dates

Throughout this book, you will see dates in parentheses after an explorer's name. These tell you when they lived. For example, "Marco Polo (1254–1324)" means that Marco Polo was born in 1254 and died in 1324.

Great explorers

Have you heard of Marco Polo, Christopher Columbus, David Livingstone, or Roald Amundsen? They were famous explorers who traveled through deserts and rainforests, over mountains, and across huge oceans and frozen lands to explore new places. They discovered places that they didn't know existed and places that nobody had ever been to before.

These explorers were often away from home for many years. They didn't have accurate maps, and they faced terrible weather, disease, and hunger. Some explorers survived using their skills or because they just refused to give up. Others died on their **expeditions**.

The explorers in this book traveled to find new lands and claim them for their countries. They went to draw new maps and to find things to trade, such as precious spices and gold. Sometimes they just went to find adventure.

Finding their way
The first explorers found their way by looking at the position of the stars and the movement of the Sun. By the 1700s, European explorers were using **navigation** instruments such as the **octant, compass**, and **telescope**.

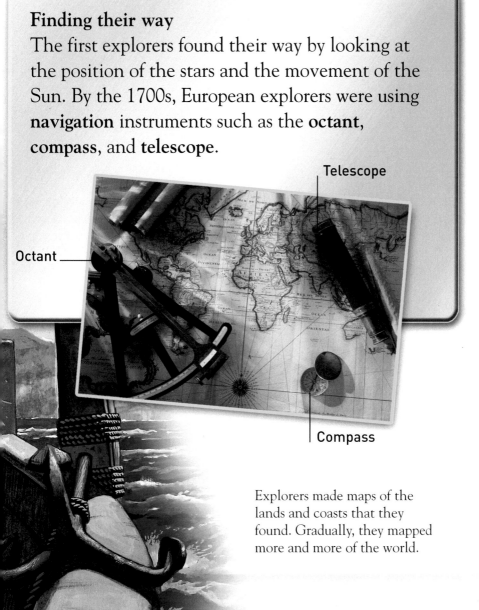

Telescope

Octant

Compass

Explorers made maps of the lands and coasts that they found. Gradually, they mapped more and more of the world.

New discoveries

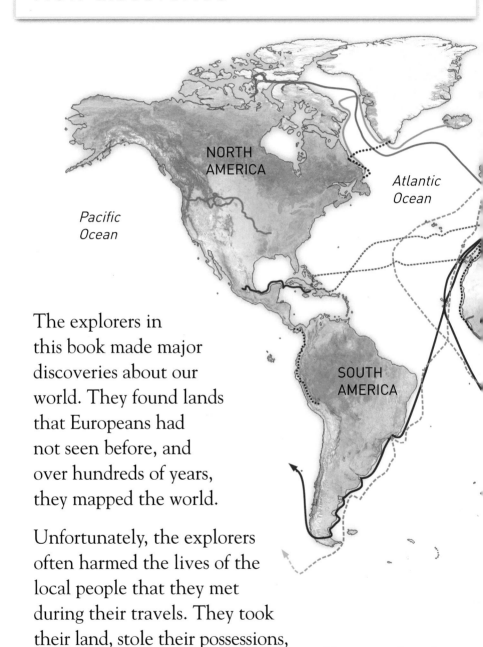

Pacific
Ocean

NORTH
AMERICA

Atlantic
Ocean

SOUTH
AMERICA

The explorers in this book made major discoveries about our world. They found lands that Europeans had not seen before, and over hundreds of years, they mapped the world.

Unfortunately, the explorers often harmed the lives of the local people that they met during their travels. They took their land, stole their possessions, and accidentally passed on diseases that killed them.

These maps show the routes of the explorers in this book.

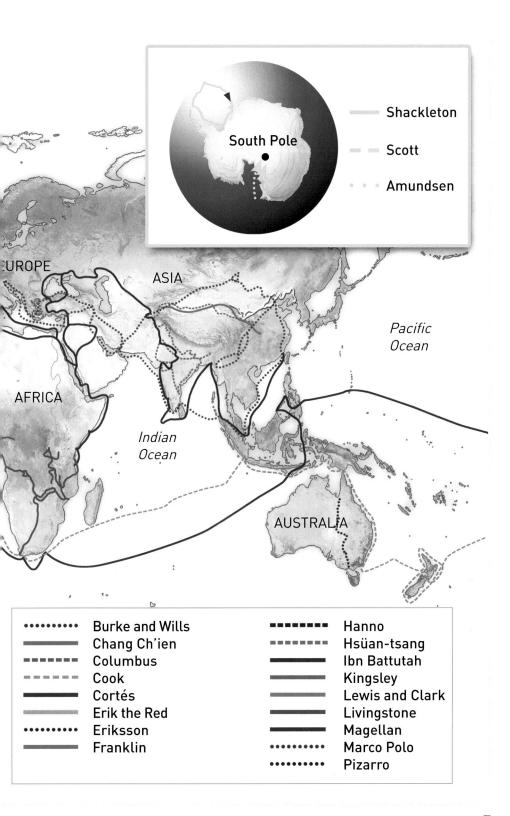

South Pole

Shackleton
Scott
Amundsen

EUROPE
ASIA

Pacific Ocean

AFRICA

Indian Ocean

AUSTRALIA

···········	Burke and Wills	▬ ▬ ▬ ▬ ▬	Hanno
▬▬▬▬	Chang Ch'ien	▬ ▬ ▬ ▬	Hsüan-tsang
▬ ▬ ▬ ▬	Columbus	▬▬▬▬	Ibn Battutah
▬ ▬ ▬ ▬	Cook	▬▬▬▬	Kingsley
▬▬▬▬	Cortés	▬▬▬▬	Lewis and Clark
▬▬▬▬	Erik the Red	▬▬▬▬	Livingstone
···········	Eriksson	▬▬▬▬	Magellan
▬▬▬▬	Franklin	···········	Marco Polo
		···········	Pizarro

7

Explorers in ancient times

Some of the first explorers that we know about were **Polynesian** people, who settled on islands in the Pacific Ocean around 3,500 years ago. They sailed across hundreds of miles of open ocean, from island to island, in big sailing canoes.

Polynesian boats had a platform in the middle to carry passengers and animals.

Chang Ch'ien
The first-known Chinese explorer was named Chang Ch'ien (200–114 BCE). In 138 BCE, he set off on a long journey west and traveled to great cities, including Rome. Ch'ien was captured by a tribe called the Huns and imprisoned for ten years before he escaped.

More than 3,000 years ago, explorers from Egypt sailed up the Nile River, searching for precious goods such as gold, spices, and perfumes to take back to Egypt.

More than 2,000 years ago, the Greeks, the Romans, and the Phoenicians all explored the lands around the Mediterranean Sea. They went to find goods to buy and sell and also to conquer new lands and build new cities.

The most famous Phoenician explorer was named Hanno. In 470 BCE, he sailed from the port of Carthage, in North Africa, down the coast of West Africa.

The Phoenicians traded goods, such as cedar wood, dyed cloth, glass, and wine, for materials such as ivory and silk.

Hsüan-tsang in India

Hsüan-tsang (602–664 CE) was a **Buddhist** monk from China. Buddhism is a religion that was founded in India about 2,500 years ago. When he was 27 years old, Hsüan-tsang made a **pilgrimage** to India in order to learn more about Buddhism.

It was a long and dangerous journey of around 1,700 miles, or mi. (3,000km), over mountains and across deserts. While crossing one desert, he ran out of water and went thirsty for five days. When he finally reached India, Hsüan-tsang visited many Buddhist **monasteries** and collected religious **manuscripts**.

In the Bamiyan valley, in Afghanistan, Hsüan-tsang was amazed by an enormous glittering statue of the Buddha, 174 ft. (53m) high. He said, "Its precious ornaments dazzle the eyes."

Hsüan-tsang translated manuscripts from India, written in a language called Sanskrit, into Chinese manuscripts such as this one, the Inga Sutra.

Hsüan-tsang returned to China 16 years after he had left. He arrived home with many horses carrying hundreds of manuscripts and religious objects that he had collected on his travels. He spent the rest of his life translating the manuscripts into Chinese and writing down the story of his amazing journey.

An endless desert

On his journey to India, Hsüan-tsang had to cross the Taklamakan Desert in western China, one of the biggest and sandiest deserts in the world. He would have had to survive hot, windy **sandstorms**. Even today, the only animals that can cross the desert and survive are camels.

Viking voyages

The Vikings lived in Scandinavia more than 1,000 years ago. They were expert shipbuilders and sailors. They sailed to Britain, France, Spain, and Russia to find new places to live and to **plunder** treasure. They also ventured out into the stormy Atlantic Ocean, where they discovered Iceland.

Viking ships were very sturdy, with space on deck for carrying goods and livestock, which the Vikings took to new lands where they settled.

Erik the Red (950–circa 1003 CE) was a famous Viking explorer. In 982 CE, Erik sailed from Iceland with his family, landed in the south of Greenland, and stayed there for three years. Erik sailed back to Iceland and then returned to Greenland with hundreds of settlers.

In about 1000 CE, Leif Eriksson, one of Erik's sons, sailed from Iceland to North America. He landed on the island of Newfoundland. He was probably the first European to land in North America.

Leif Eriksson lands in North America after crossing the Atlantic Ocean.

Sun compass
Viking sailors might have used a wooden dial like this, called a sun compass, to check the direction in which to sail. Most of the time, Vikings stayed in sight of the coast and went ashore at night.

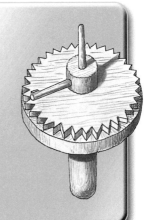

Marco Polo in China

Marco Polo (1254–1324) was born in Venice, in Italy. In 1271, when he was just 17 years old, he set off for China with his father and his uncle. They took gifts for Kublai Khan, the powerful ruler of China in the 1200s CE.

Marco Polo crossed high mountains in Afghanistan on his way to China.

We don't know the exact route that Marco Polo took, but in Asia, they followed an old trading route called the **Silk Road**. In 1275, four years after setting off, they arrived at the court of Kublai Khan.

The Polos at the palace of Kublai Khan.

Kublai Khan sent Marco Polo to different parts of his huge empire in order to bring back information about the people who lived there. Marco was Kublai Khan's spy.

Marco Polo's group stayed in China for 17 years before a three-year voyage home to Venice, returning in 1295. He had been away for so long that his family and friends thought he was dead, so they were amazed to see him.

Amazing sights
In China, Marco Polo saw things that he had never seen before, including kites and fireworks. He also saw paper money for the first time and wrote, "With these pieces of paper, they can buy anything."

Marco Polo must have crossed the Great Wall of China on his travels. At the time, the wall was smaller and made of earth and stones.

Ibn Battutah

In 1325, a **Muslim** man named Ibn Battutah (1304–1369) left his home in Morocco. He was heading for Mecca, a holy city for Muslims, which is in modern-day Saudi Arabia. During the 3,000-mi. (5,000-km) journey, Ibn Battutah grew to love traveling. So instead of going home after visiting Mecca, he went exploring in what is now Iraq and Iran and along the coast of Africa.

In Africa, Ibn Battutah saw hippopotamuses for the first time. He wrote that they looked like horses.

Ibn Battutah crossed the Sahara Desert in a **caravan** of camels.

Ibn Battutah traveled on the Nile River, possibly on a dhow (a type of sailboat) like this.

Ibn Battutah then went to visit Sultan Muhammad of Delhi, one of the richest men in India, who asked him to take gifts to the Chinese ruler in Beijing. Ibn Battutah was amazed by the bustling Chinese cities that he saw on his journey, but a war kept him from reaching Beijing, and he decided that it was time to go home.

Columbus and the Americas

Christopher Columbus (1451–1506) was a trader from Genoa, in Italy, who is famous for being the first European to discover the Americas.

The king and queen of Spain wanted new **colonies**, so they paid Columbus to go on an expedition. Columbus was sure that if he sailed far enough into the Atlantic Ocean, he would reach Asia. He didn't know that North and South America lay between Europe and Asia.

Columbus's three ships were the *Santa Maria* (the biggest), the *Niña*, and the *Pinta*.

Columbus set off in 1492 with three small ships. They sailed for a month but didn't see any land. Finally, after 35 days at sea, they saw an island. Columbus thought that he'd succeeded in getting to Asia. But he had actually found one of the islands that are now called the Bahamas.

Columbus went ashore in the Bahamas and claimed the new land for Spain.

Life at sea
Altogether there were about 90 men on Columbus's three little ships. Columbus had a small cabin, but the crew slept on deck, wherever they could find a space. They ate hard biscuits, dried meat, and any fish that they could catch.

Cortés and Pizarro

The lands that Christopher Columbus found in 1492 became known to Europeans as the New World, because they didn't know that these lands had existed before. For Europeans, there were two whole new **continents** to explore. Dozens of European expeditions crossed the Atlantic Ocean to claim the land and find riches.

In 1519, Hernando Cortés (1485–1547), from Spain, went looking for a group of people called the Aztecs, who lived in Mexico. He marched through the jungle and found the Aztec capital city, called Tenochtitlán.

This picture shows Aztec warriors defending the temple of Tenochtitlán against Cortés and his men.

Hernando Cortés traveled with hundreds of armed soldiers.

Francisco Pizarro captured the Inca ruler, Atahualpa, and demanded gold as a ransom for his release.

Cortés and his men were amazed by the size of the city. They defeated the Aztecs in battle in 1521, destroyed the city, and took all the gold they could find back to Spain.

The promise of gold encouraged other Spanish explorers. Francisco Pizarro (1471–1541) ventured down the west coast of South America. He discovered the Inca people of Peru, conquered them, and plundered their treasure.

Inca treasure

Chocolate and tomatoes

The explorers who visited the Americas found plants that nobody in Europe had ever seen or tasted. They included cocoa (used to make chocolate), tomatoes, potatoes, corn, chili peppers, and peanuts.

First around the world

Portuguese adventurer Ferdinand Magellan (1480–1521) was the first explorer to sail around South America to reach the Pacific Ocean. Magellan set off from Spain in 1519 with five ships and 260 men. He sailed down to the southern tip of South America and found a passage through to the Pacific Ocean, now called the Strait of Magellan.

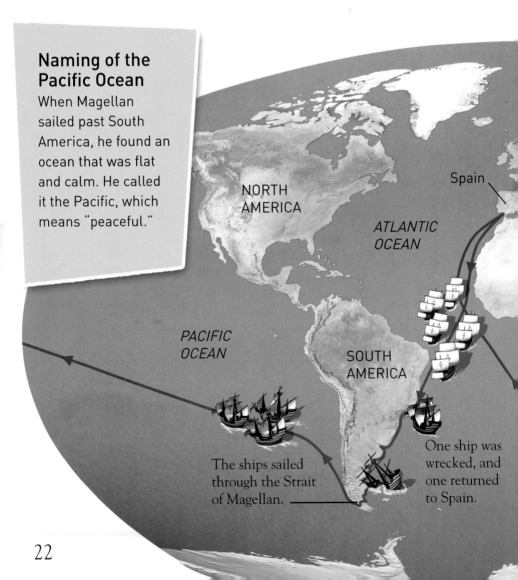

Naming of the Pacific Ocean

When Magellan sailed past South America, he found an ocean that was flat and calm. He called it the Pacific, which means "peaceful."

NORTH AMERICA

ATLANTIC OCEAN

Spain

PACIFIC OCEAN

SOUTH AMERICA

The ships sailed through the Strait of Magellan.

One ship was wrecked, and one returned to Spain.

Magellan thought it would take a few days to cross the Pacific Ocean. It took months. Magellan's men ran out of fresh food, and many of them died from **malnutrition** and disease. Magellan threw his maps into the sea in despair, yet they still reached the Philippines.

In the Philippines, Magellan was killed in a fight with local people, but one of his ships reached Spain in 1522. It was the first boat to sail all the way around the world.

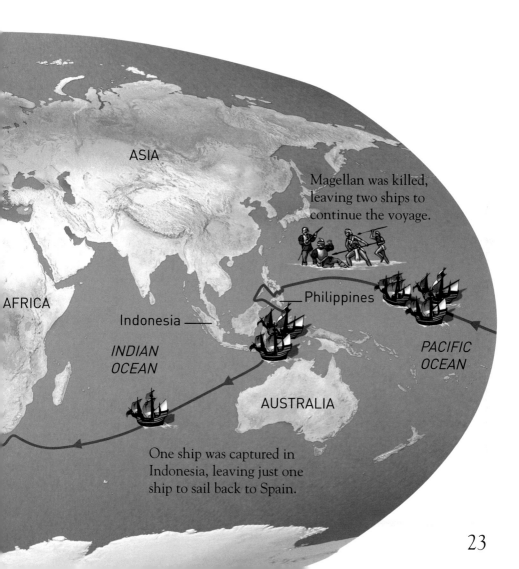

ASIA

Magellan was killed, leaving two ships to continue the voyage.

AFRICA

Philippines

Indonesia

INDIAN OCEAN

PACIFIC OCEAN

AUSTRALIA

One ship was captured in Indonesia, leaving just one ship to sail back to Spain.

Cook in the Pacific

James Cook (1728–1779) was a captain in the British navy. In 1768, the British government sent Cook to search for a continent in the southern part of the Pacific Ocean. Cook sailed a long way south but found nothing. He then sailed around New Zealand and Australia, drawing accurate maps of the coastlines.

Cook's party explored the east coast of Australia.

James Cook took scientists and artists on his expeditions to record the landscapes, people, animals, and plants that they found.

On his next voyage, he sailed as far south as he could before his ships were stopped by frozen seas. We now know that this ice was surrounding the continent of Antarctica.

On his third voyage, Cook's men became the first Europeans to land on the islands of Hawaii, where Cook died in 1779. He was stabbed to death by locals in an argument over a stolen boat.

Cook carried a very precise watch that allowed him to figure out his exact **longitude** and make accurate maps.

This is a modern replica of Cook's ship the *Endeavour*, which he took on his first voyage.

Lewis and Clark

In 1804, Meriwether Lewis (1774–1809) and William Clark (1770–1838) traveled all the way across North America to reach the Pacific Ocean.

The United States government wanted to **survey** the northwestern United States and find a route to the west coast of North America. They chose Lewis and Clark for the job. The two explorers set out from Saint Louis in May of 1804 with 43 soldiers. Over the summer, they paddled up the Missouri River in canoes and then built a log cabin to stay in over the winter.

Seeing the sea
When William Clark saw the Pacific Ocean in 1805, he said, "Great joy in the camp. We are in view of the ocean."

Lewis and Clark canoed along rivers
because it was faster than going over land.

They set off again in the spring.
The hardest part of their expedition
was finding a way through the Rocky
Mountains. A **Native American**
woman named Sacagawea, who knew
some mountain passes, helped them.
They eventually reached the Pacific
Ocean in the fall of 1805.

Lewis and Clark, with
Sacagawea, reach the Great
Falls on the Missouri River.

The Northwest Passage

About 500 years ago, explorers began searching for the Northwest Passage—a water route around the north of America. Traveling there is difficult and dangerous. The ocean is frozen all winter, and there is a maze of islands to navigate through.

In 1845, Englishman John Franklin (1786–1847) set off with two ships, HMS *Erebus* and HMS *Terror*, and 128 men to find the Northwest Passage. Two years later, they hadn't come back, so a search party was sent. The rescuers found Franklin's ships stuck in the ice. The crews had run out of food, and Franklin had died in 1847. His men had tried to walk south to safety but had all died too.

Amundsen finds a way

It was Norwegian explorer Roald Amundsen (see page 36) who finally found the Northwest Passage. Between 1903 and 1906, he sailed along it in a small boat with just six men and six dogs.

28

Franklin's last message
In 1859, a search party found a note buried in a pile of stones on King William Island, in the Northwest Passage. The note was written by Franklin's men, and it reported Franklin's death in 1847.

Franklin's goggles were found by the search party in an abandoned boat.

Franklin and his crew had to abandon their ships in the Arctic wastes. With their ships gone, they had little chance of survival.

Mary Kingsley in Africa

When she was a little girl, Mary Kingsley (1862–1900) loved reading books about Africa. When her parents died, she decided to go see Africa for herself. She wanted to meet the African people, study the plants and animals, and find adventure.

Kingsley didn't have any special clothes for exploring. Instead, she wore what most English women wore at the time: a long skirt and a blouse with a high neck. She always carried an umbrella and took fishhooks, tobacco, and cloth to trade for food and other things she needed. She traveled with help from local people.

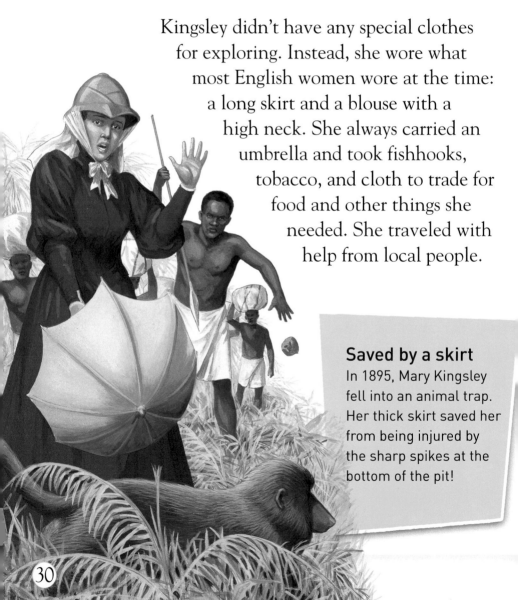

Saved by a skirt

In 1895, Mary Kingsley fell into an animal trap. Her thick skirt saved her from being injured by the sharp spikes at the bottom of the pit!

Mary Kingsley exploring along the
Ogowe River in Gabon in about 1895.

On her travels, Kingsley collected fish from African
rivers for the British Museum, some of which were
named after her.

The Water Babies

Mary's father, Charles Kingsley,
wrote a famous book called *The
Water Babies*, about a boy who
goes on adventures around the
world. Mary must have read it.
She couldn't wait to go on her
own adventures.

Livingstone in Africa

Many explorers from Europe went to Africa in the 1800s. David Livingstone (1813–1873) was one of the most famous. Livingstone traveled to Africa in 1840 to be a **missionary**. He set up two missions in southern Africa, but he found that he enjoyed exploring more than missionary work.

Livingstone's first taste of exploration was in 1849, when he crossed the Kalahari Desert. In 1855, he traveled down the great Zambezi River and discovered the towering Victoria Falls.

Livingstone was the first European to look over Victoria Falls, on the Zambezi River. He named the waterfall after the British queen.

David Livingstone meets Henry Morton Stanley in Africa in 1871.

In 1866, Livingstone began hunting for the source of the Nile River. Nobody heard from him for years, and search parties were sent to look for him. Henry Morton Stanley, a reporter for the *New York Herald* newspaper, finally found him in 1871, but he couldn't persuade Livingstone to leave Africa with him. Livingstone died of malaria, a tropical disease spread by mosquitoes, in 1873.

Livingstone's last expedition
Livingstone became sick during his search for the source of the Nile River, and his helpers carried him through the swamps. When he died, two helpers took his body 1,000 mi. (1,600km) to the coast.

Across Australia

Australians Robert O'Hara Burke (1821–1861) and William John Wills (1834–1861) led the first expedition to cross the continent of Australia from south to north. Burke and Wills set off from Melbourne in 1860 with 19 men. They set up a camp at a place called Cooper Creek. Then Burke, Wills, John King, and Charlie Grey continued northward.

The four men struggled through thick forests and baking-hot deserts. After 57 days, they reached the north coast of Australia. They turned back for home, but hunger, bad weather, and illness slowed them down, and Grey died. They finally staggered back to Cooper Creek, but the other members of the expedition were gone. Burke and Wills died at Cooper Creek. John King lived with a group of **Aboriginal people** until he was rescued months later.

Camel transportation

Burke and Wills left Melbourne with two years' worth of supplies, 23 horses, six wagons, and 26 camels. The camels were brought from India and chosen because they could survive in hot deserts.

Burke, Wills, and King were exhausted and sick when they got back to Cooper Creek.

Amundsen in the Antarctic

Roald Amundsen (1872–1928) was a Norwegian explorer. He led the first expedition ever to reach the South Pole.

In 1910, Amundsen sailed to Antarctica on his sturdy ship, the *Fram*. He set off from his base on the coast of Antarctica in October 1911, at the beginning of the summer. He took four sleds, pulled by teams of dogs.

Amundsen's ship, the *Fram*, was built to stand up to the thick **pack ice**.

Local skills

Between 1905 and 1908, Amundsen lived and traveled in the Arctic. He learned many skills from the local Inuit people, such as making clothes from furs and driving teams of sled dogs. These skills helped him reach the South Pole.

Amundsen planted a Norwegian flag at the South Pole and then turned back for home.

Amundsen and his men struggled for weeks over mountains and glaciers. He finally reached the South Pole on December 14, 1911. British explorer Robert Falcon Scott got there just 34 days later. (See page 38 for more about Scott.)

Dog teams pulled Amundsen across the ice and snow.

Scott and Shackleton

In 1911–1912, British explorer Robert Falcon Scott (1868–1912) and four other men walked 800 mi. (1,300km) to the South Pole, only to find that Roald Amundsen had beaten them to it. On the way back, the men slowly ran out of food. Two men died from exhaustion and **frostbite**. Scott and the other two struggled on but were trapped in their tent by a storm, where they died. They were just 11 mi. (18km) from a food station, where they would have been safe.

Scott and his team pose for a photograph with Amundsen's Norwegian flag.

Antarctic food
Pemmican was a high-energy food that Scott and Amundsen both took for their expeditions. It was made with dried meat and fat and was often used to make a stew called "hoosh."

Shackleton's men launching the *James Caird*, in which
Shackleton sailed to the island of South Georgia to get help.

In 1915, the ship of another British Antarctic explorer,
Ernest Shackleton (1874–1922), was crushed by sea ice.
Shackleton and his men then drifted on **ice floes** for
five months before using boats salvaged from the ship to
escape to an island. Then Shackleton and a few others
sailed 800 mi. (1,300km) across the ocean to get help.
After nine months in total, all of his men were saved.

An ice floe near
Elephant Island,
Antarctica, where
Shackleton's men
survived for four
months while
Shackleton
went for help.

Norgay and Hillary

Tenzing Norgay (1914–1986) and Edmund Hillary (1919–2008) were the first explorers to climb to the summit of Mount Everest, the highest mountain in the world. Mount Everest is in the Himalayas. It is called Chomolungma by local people, which means "Holy Mother." It is 29,029 ft. (8,848m) high.

Tenzing and Hillary on Everest's summit

Oxygen equipment
High on Everest, the air is very thin, which makes it hard to breathe, especially when doing exercise such as climbing. Tenzing and Hillary took oxygen in bottles and breathed it through masks.

Edmund Hillary
(left) and
Tenzing Norgay
(right) after
descending
safely from
the summit

Tenzing Norgay was a local man called a Sherpa.
He was an expert mountaineer and helped carry
equipment up the mountain. Edmund Hillary
was from New Zealand. They were part of a large
expedition and were chosen to make an attempt
on the summit. They reached their goal at 11:30
in the morning on May 29, 1953. They had
succeeded where many climbers had failed before,
and they soon became world-famous.

The route that
Tenzing and
Hillary took to
the summit of
Mount Everest

Armstrong on the Moon

American astronaut Neil Armstrong (1930–2012) was the first person to stand on the surface of another world—the Moon. Armstrong was commander of the *Apollo 11* spacecraft, which flew to the Moon in 1969. The other crew members were Edwin "Buzz" Aldrin and Michael Collins.

It took two days to travel to the Moon. Collins stayed in the **command module**, while Armstrong and Aldrin descended to the Moon's surface in the **lunar module**. Their fuel supply got dangerously low as they searched for a place to land, but Armstrong stayed calm and got down safely. A few hours later, wearing a space suit, Armstrong stepped carefully onto the Moon's dusty surface.

Apollo 11 was launched into space by a giant Saturn V rocket.

On the surface

When Armstrong stepped onto the Moon, he said the now-famous words, "That's one small step for man, one giant leap for mankind." Back on Earth, there was great excitement about the Moon landings. Around 500 million people were watching as Armstrong took his historic steps.

Armstrong and Aldrin set up experiments, took photographs, and collected rocks to take back to Earth.

The astronauts clambered down a ladder onto the Moon's surface.

Modern exploration

There are still many undiscovered places in the world. On the Yucatán Peninsula in Mexico, there are huge networks of underwater caves. These cave networks are like mazes, and divers have to be careful not to get lost. In these caves, scientists have discovered types of animals found nowhere else on the planet.

These divers are exploring amazing underwater caverns on the Yucatán Peninsula in Mexico.

The ocean floor is another place that people have hardly explored. Some parts are thousands of feet underwater, which is too deep for most submarines to reach.

In March of 2012, the **submersible** *Deepsea Challenger* reached the bottom of the Challenger Deep, nearly 7 mi. (11km) under the Pacific Ocean and the deepest point in all of Earth's seabeds. The pilot was movie director James Cameron, who spent three hours exploring the ocean floor before returning to the surface.

Robotic submersibles have allowed us to explore the deep ocean landscape and the creatures that live there.

Space exploration
The Moon is the farthest that human explorers have reached into space. In the future, astronauts may visit Mars. Until then, robot **space probes** such as *Opportunity*, which landed on Mars in 2004, are exploring the amazing solar system for us.

Glossary

Aboriginal people the Australian Aboriginal people are the original inhabitants of Australia

BCE Before the Common Era (any date before 1 CE)

Buddhist a person who follows Buddhism (a religion founded by the Buddha)

caravan a group of traders or pilgrims traveling across a desert

CE the Common Era (any date after 1 CE)

colony land that is claimed and settled by another country

command module the section of spacecraft that the astronauts left and returned to Earth in

compass a navigational instrument with a magnetic needle that always points north

continent Earth's areas of land that are separated by water are called continents, usually referring to Africa, Antarctica, Asia, Australia, Europe, North America, and South America

expedition a journey that is taken for a special purpose such as to explore a place

frostbite damage, normally to fingers, toes, and the nose, caused by exposure to extremely cold temperatures

ice floe a large sheet of floating sea ice

longitude an imaginary line around Earth from the North Pole to the South Pole, used to measure distances

lunar module the section of spacecraft that took astronauts between the command module and the Moon's surface

malnutrition a lack of proper nutrition, caused by not eating enough food or by having an unhealthy diet

manuscript a book or other document written by hand

missionary a person on a mission to try to spread their religion

Muslim a person who follows Islam (one of the world's oldest and most followed religions)

monasteries the place where a group of religious people (usually monks) lives and practices their religion

Native American an original inhabitant of North or South America

navigation planning the course of a journey and finding the way

octant a navigational instrument used to measure the height of stars from a moving ship

pack ice large pieces of sea ice that have been squeezed together

pilgrimage a journey to a place that is sacred to a religion such as Mecca for Muslims

plunder to steal using force

Polynesian a person from an area of the Pacific Ocean that includes Hawaii, Samoa, and the Cook Islands

sandstorm a strong wind carrying clouds of sand and dust

Silk Road an ancient trading route between China and eastern Europe, named after the silk that was transported along the route

space probe a robotic spacecraft sent to another planet or moon to take photographs and collect scientific information

submersible a small submarine used for scientific research or underwater exploration that can work in waters that are too deep for divers

survey to complete a map or detailed view of an area of land

telescope a navigational instrument used to make objects appear closer

Index

If you have enjoyed reading
this book, look out for more in
the Kingfisher Readers series!

**Collect
and read
them all!**

KINGFISHER READERS: LEVEL 4

The Arctic and Antarctica ☐
Flight ☐
Human Body ☐
Pirates ☐
Rivers ☐
Sharks ☐
Weather ☐

KINGFISHER READERS: LEVEL 5

Ancient Egyptians ☐
Explorers ☐
Hurricanes ☐
Rainforests ☐
Record Breakers—The Fastest ☐
Record Breakers—The Most Dangerous ☐
Space ☐

For a full list of Kingfisher Readers books, plus
guidance for teachers and parents and activities
and fun stuff for kids, go to the Kingfisher Readers
website: www.kingfisherreaders.com

31901055400222